what are
MOMS
made of?

Written by Ruth Austin · Designed by Jill Labieniec

Moms like you are made of little things, gathered all together...

_____

_____

_____

_____

_____

With love, _____

*It's not one single quality
or one big event that
makes you the wonderful
mom you are.*

It's the example of motherhood you put forward every day. It's in the fleeting moments and the little actions: the small trials, the big triumphs, the shared joys, the sacrifices, and the laughter. It's all that you're made of, all that you do and give—and it means so very much.

What are moms made of?

*Boundless affection mixed
with kindness and care,*

Comfort and joy, and stories to share.

*Sunny dreams of the future.
Hard work and delight.*

That's what moms are made of.

What else are moms made of?

*Sprinklings of silliness,
celebrations, and fun,*

*Laughing through chaos
and getting stuff done.*

Mishaps made better with support and with strength,

That's what moms are made of.

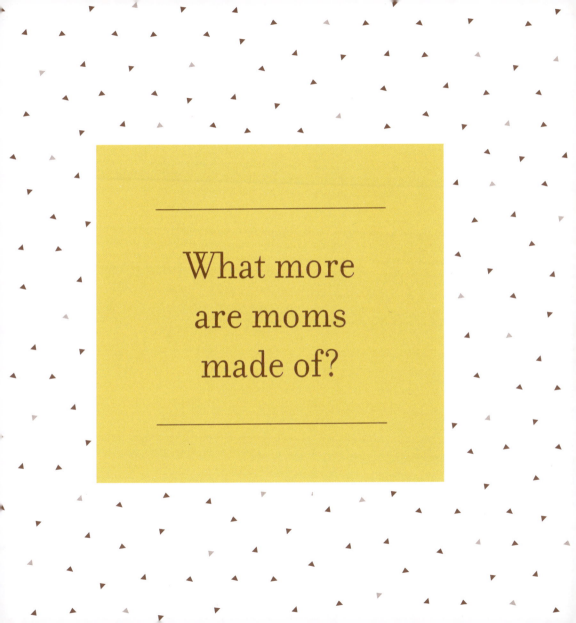

*Full-hearted hugs
from two generous arms,*

*Grace under pressure and
know-how and calm.*

Patience—with lots of encouragement too.

That's what moms are made of.

What are moms really made of?

*Watching time fly and
a few sleepless nights,*

*Long heart-to-heart talks
that set everything right.*

*Those magical words
that show the right way,*

That's what moms are made of.

How do you
know what moms
are made of?

*All the minutes and the
hours spent soothing tears,*

*So many small moments
adding up through the years...*

Dedication and guidance and, above all, love.

You're all the best things moms are made of.

With special thanks to the entire Compendium family.

CREDITS:
Written by: Ruth Austin
Designed by: Jill Labieniec
Edited by: Amelia Riedler

Library of Congress Control Number: 2017942874
ISBN: 978-1-943200-70-2

© 2017 by Compendium, Inc. All rights reserved. No part of this publication may be reproduced or transmitted in any form or by any means, electronic or mechanical, including photocopy, recording, or any storage and retrieval system now known or to be invented without written permission from the publisher. Contact: Compendium, Inc., 2100 North Pacific Street, Seattle, WA 98103. *What Are Moms Made Of?*; Compendium; live inspired; and the format, design, layout, and coloring used in this book are trademarks and/or trade dress of Compendium, Inc. This book may be ordered directly from the publisher, but please try your local bookstore first. Call us at 800.91.IDEAS, or come see our full line of inspiring products at live-inspired.com.

1st printing. Printed in China with soy and metallic inks.